Rain

Rain

A DIARY OF SAMAIRA SINGH

BlueRose Publishers
New Delhi • London

First Published in January 2022

ISBN: 978-93-5472-801-3

BLUEROSE PUBLISHERS
www.bluerosepublishers.com
info@bluerosepublishers.com
+91 8882 898 898

Cover Design:
Muskan Sachdeva

Typographic Design:
Ilma Mirza

Distributed by: BlueRose, Amazon, Flipkart

To my cat Tintin, whose eyes have a spark that I perceive in none another.

And if thou gaze long into an abyss, the abyss will also gaze into thee.

— Friedrich Nietzsche

TO THE READER

Most people conceive depression as sadness and regard it as an insignificant mental illness. To contradict this viewpoint, I argue that depression is more than grief, sorrow and physical suffering.

Depression in its severe form, i.e., major depression or simply depression, in the branch of psychiatry, is a grave disorder of the mind, which if left untreated, would lead to atrocious outcomes.

Depression is like a blackhole made up of thoughts in the mind, which within a span of time pulls and consumes the mind with distress. Depression feeds upon the mind, depletes the person's self-image and their respect for themselves.

In many cases, people have encountered such traumatizing events that they find it difficult to suppress painful memories into the unconscious mind. They are unable to process the past, that is, past thoughts, which may be unwanted or persistent. Many ruminate the depressive thoughts, which leads their mental state to grow worse and consequently gives rise to depression.

Depression is distress caused without an apparent cause. People suffering from it are not only battling with a mental illness, but also with themselves.

Depression is more common in young adults and teenagers. Depressed individuals may start to oversleep or experience early awakening, while others barely get sufficient sleep or suffer from insomnia and regard it as normal when it's not. They get fatigued easily and despite exercise and a good diet, nothing benefits, as depression is a disorder of the mind and not the body; the mind is impaired to such a range that the physical body is also impaired. In most cases, people around the depressed individuals do not manifest any worry for them and have no idea what is going on underneath.

Depressed individuals see their life as a burden, and they feel as if nobody deserves the kind of treatment they receive. Eventually, they cannot devise reasons why they should continue on with their lives. It may lead them to practice self-harm or suicide. They feel that ending their lives is the only option left.

Before attempting any form of self-harm or suicide, they may start to utter 'goodbye' or seem more relieved than usual or their behavior is completely different and changed. They feel as if the end is near.

Many depressed individuals have been taunted and judged. As a result, out of fear, they choose not to share their intents with anyone. They don't trust for the medication or the counselling to yield any benefit. They believe that with time, it would pass, when it does not. Most are indifferent to the symptoms of depression.

For physical diseases, much heed is given and immediate care is provided. Whereas, hardly any attention and concern is given to mental illness. As a result, depressed ones are rarely paid heed to and the cases go unacknowledged.

Depression resolves within months or is chronic or lifelong, and we must bear in mind that the symptoms of depression may diminish or grow worse with time. In many cases, time cannot aid a dire illness like depression, which requires medical care, heed and attention. We must strive to seek help for mental health at the earliest.

A significant cause of depression and self-harm among teens is cyberbullying and online harassment. Teenagers are at the greatest peril to become victims as well as predators of cyberbullying, as they become captives of the internet.

Many teens are at a frail age while their inner-self is still developing. To see such abominable messages online has an abject impact both on their emotional and physical well-being.

The internet has no comprehension of right and wrong. You cannot meet people online as they are far away but not farther than the chat which brings them near to you. You can forget words said by someone in real life, but the traumatizing words on the internet stay there. Those words remain and rest on the screen and your mind forever.

On the internet, nobody cares or thinks before pressing the send button or how these messages will lead to disastrous consequences, to such an extent that it can cost someone's life. And hardly any action is taken against cyberbullying.

The internet is boundless. It is not confined. It has no real restrictions.

SAMAIRA

EXORDIUM

Death of all miseries, birth of happiness.

The joyful February mourns in October. Words have piercing edges, as sharp as needles. So I deem, how can mere words have tragic consequences? They're just words…

JUNE

You can bear demise, but you cannot bear extreme torture. Yet you may, by choosing the act of death by your will.

11 JULY, 2021

SUNDAY

T HE notification tone of my laptop broke through the silence. It was from *Wish*. I was expecting some e-mail from someone but to my dismay, only an e-mail from a shop had come. Why would I expect anything when there's nothing left to expect from? I've already lost everything. 'Does it matter?' I thought to myself.

The last god-awful, terrible-as-anything week was spent in patience. My old journal had got full, so I waited for a new one to arrive. In the meantime, I collected new ideas for my poetry.

My new diary arrived. The cover shows Vincent van Gogh's painting, and his paintings are simply extraordinary.

I didn't get any sleep last night. I stayed up the whole night due to an unknown reason, probably insomnia. My parents barely notice if I'm alive or something, so I think I'm better off without them.

When I touch my chest, I feel a usual sensation. A very, very big heaviness I feel inside. It descends me straight to the bottom, and I never want to get up from there.

I have been in this abyss for too long, stranded and holding on to the rope without any hope. I'm at the bottom depth now of this abyss. I don't know if there's surface beneath me. It's the never-ending tale of my severe depression. It's completely dark and hollow.

I'm descending downwards, and I don't see any brightness at the end either. It's just plain, complete jet-black darkness. This abyss is made up of nothing but thoughts, it's not physically there. All it has is shadows and thoughts of just one person— *him.*

And it wouldn't matter if I moved on right now. I shall always love him.

9:41 am

It was a relief to get all my work— the awful work— done, just to come to you and so I did. Who else would I go to when I was so lonely?

By some chance perhaps, I made it through June. And June was the month to which I had doubts of surviving. So don't know how, didn't die, even though died mentally.

One minute my father and I are good, the next minute he's yelling at me again. Story of my life. Same with my mother, she receives all the enjoyment and I all the torment. She can't get away with this nonsense of hers.

I have not been sleeping at night for the past five days and it's not something new to me. I'm used to it.

Today is finally Saturday. In my free time, I'll learn how to make an omelet because I think it's easy. Also, I'm so sick of this sleeping schedule of mine. Yesterday, I slept for ten hours in the daytime. My sleep cycle has become disgusting, just like me. And I have become thin, almost—emaciated. My hands are so, so, so thin.

Ugh. My sleep cycle is horrible. I wish I could sleep and slowly disappear… from the world and the people. Then I wouldn't have to receive any kind of torment ever. I just want to drift away from reality, into my dreamland and never ever want to be judged, used and ill-treated again. I want to cuddle with my pillows and never want to wake up when I go to sleep.

The sun is too painful.

12:17 pm

All to hang on to is time.

This week I had been sleeping throughout the afternoon.

I wonder when there shall come a time when my chest feels light and free. I don't think that's going to happen.

'Yet in the end I didn't have the strength to take a decision.' Over the months, no matter what, despite everything, I didn't take a decision at the end. Neither could I hate *him* nor could I take a decision, and I don't know if that will cost me in the future.

I was like a tortoise, too scared to show itself. So, I hid and fell into a shell of denial and delusions. It was better in there.

Today, I had a really good time spent with my mother. If I'd describe her in a word, I would say *'oblivious'*, father as *'short-tempered'* and brother as *'a pure psychopath'*. That's what I would call them.

3:30 pm

I'll sleep without any concern if I'll wake up tomorrow or not, as I feel this slight pressure in my chest and it's got me incapacitated. It almost feels as if my lungs have frozen. They are aching. I wonder if the last thing I could get would be a heart attack. But why not, my heart has already suffered severe damages and injuries. It's the same thing any way.

12 JULY, 2021

MONDAY

Time is tormented, thus, some of the few gains of sleeping can be that you escape the time with peaceful sleep.

I looked at the clock and saw different numbers. I imagined being the hand of time and the numbers being different people. That is, as the hand of time (me) progress, I meet different numbers (people). As time advances, I'll be moved on to the next number (person).

The hand of time always moves on to the next number (one to twelve). And thus, so many people shall come into my life.

But what if the hand of time (me) has frozen to a single number, a single person? Even when it tries to move, some force pushes the hand back to that single number (person) only.

I was stranded in the past. I wasn't going on. The hand never moved from there and was always stuck to that single number (person).

9:00 am

Finally, when I was at rest, I started to think of *him*. As it seemed, the daily dose of the delusions became a torture and relief simultaneously. But it was more of relief.

I would never have the strength to erase him from my mind.

Something which couldn't be yielded by reality, I yielded it by my imagination. I couldn't give upon *those* memories now, be it distressing ones, his image was all that I needed. But all his memories started to blur with the advancing hand of time. I was forgetting him a little now, which I didn't want to.

3:00 pm

O I long for someone to read my diary. Well— no, I would never allow that as I have always been a private person. It was too onerous to express my feelings without being laughed at or judged. I'd rather die than share my innermost problems and feelings to someone. I always kept it all to myself.

I was like this cloud— I'd fly high above the grounds of reality. Then I wouldn't have to look at the war or injustice below. I wandered here and there and when I rained (wept), I faded a little bit.

Lovers were as clouds, progressing in their own way— but if a catastrophe struck, a turbulent thunder would induce.

20 JULY, 2021

TUESDAY

As soon as the sun made its way through the cloudy sky, I was empty. June… July… empty. The hurt subsided and the emptiness emerged. Seven months of pain and now I was finally vacant.

For all I knew, being empty was a thousand times more peaceful than being in distress. Why? Because the pain was unbearable. This way it was bearable, in a way.

I couldn't process an emotion anymore as my mind was utterly befogged, as if it was deeply frosted with ice.

All the months my heart waited for you, poor heart, it has died now.

1:37 pm

When I'm doing nothing, I just write new poems. They are written from my imagination, not my heart. It wasn't my heart which was afflicted— it was my mind, due to the memory and the thoughts.

My mother served me coffee. I took it from her hand and replied, "Thank you." Then I sat in the balcony, staring blankly at the coffee mug. *He* was... fading. I couldn't handle it. *The pain goes, he goes.*

I was like a balloon, burst by a needle. I could never fly high again.

2:06 pm

I finished most of my work and then retired to you.
It's July now and each month seems like a day.

I have come so far in the journey of words. I couldn't yet say I was happy— the aches were alleviated by time but not vanished, as pain once induced in life could be avoided but could never be forgotten; it stayed with you forever.

5:50 pm

I looked in the mirror, stared at my face without any reason and made a braid out of the messed hair. I washed my hair regularly, but in no time, they seemed to get rough again.

While tying up my hair, I thought about going downstairs. But before that, I made myself an omelet and a coffee. I wasn't good at cooking; all I knew to cook was noodles and omelet.

I peeked out of my window and gazed at the group of girls and boys. I wanted to make friends really bad, so I led myself down the stairs.

I was myself the biggest coward I'd ever known. When I had seen them, I tried to approach them. But when some boys started to come towards me, out of fear, I turned my head away and ran back home.

It was wrong for me to play a dumb coward like this, but what was the point? They would not take much time to dislike me.

I was always afraid of teenagers. I thought I'd say the wrong word. I felt as if people were out to get me. I thought everybody would judge me.

Having friends lead to a healthy life and I had none. And not only was I alone continuously, but also, I'd become mentally unstable.

And after I'd seen the text in front of my eyes, written on the screen *'you should die,'* I felt like I wasn't allowed to live anymore; I just wanted to rip off each and every single part of my skin.

22 JULY, 2021

THURSDAY

Everything to be done is just a mere question of time. My mother can tell by my expression that I look confused. I clearly didn't know how things should proceed.

The last winter had left pretty much everything in ruins, I loved you then, yet this winter, I suspected you. And my own thoughts led me down to a road of catastrophe.

I sat in my room for a while and wondered why people smoked to alleviate their pains. To fix a bad thing, by a bad thing. I was underaged to smoke but if I had the chance, I'd try once. I thought it would be fun.

There were cigarettes in my washroom. So I went there and tried to light one. But then I stood still— it was pointless. *Smoking kills.... not instantly.*

So I left the cigarette right where it was and retired back to my room, sighing.

1:16 pm

Going back to my love was like going to sleep after a weary day, where every resistance would fail.

Today I dreamt of *him* and it was so real. I saw him walking away— away from me. I followed his footsteps and when he was farther away, I cried his name as I had no other option. I was terrified. He looked back to see who it was and I hid. I was too afraid of my action, so I kept hiding while he walked away.

What I was thinking when I had woken up was:

Fear ends love.

2:00 pm

It didn't make sense but in a way it did: If you'd fall from a short height, you'd survive. But if you'd fall from a higher one, you'd be severely injured or maybe even dead. Same in love, time spent together builds the height. The more you love, the more the height, the more the harm.
Good heavens! I was badly hurt.

'Hope' was the planet Pluto and I were on earth.
Depression loved me and life had abandoned me.

I saw my life as a building collapsing, and the only force which saved me from ruin was *fear*.

For me, love was a clean glass of water. Outward forces made it foul, whereas attachment made the water mixed with alcohol. All these things made the same fluid.

4:16 pm

Finally, I searched online on the subject, 'what to do when you feel empty.' The steps were pretty simple. They went as follows—

1. Get outside

For what? I don't have any friends and the weather is too hot anyway.

2. Sort through your emotions

Which one? I feel one emotion that's it— sadness.

3. Meditate

No. I'm too tired to get out of the bed.

4. Reach out to a friend

Who? My cat? He can barely make sense of what I'm saying.

5. Listen to music

Music makes me feel even more overwhelmed.

6. Try some chores

I don't know how to put the cap of the toothpaste after brushing with it.

7. Check in with your needs

I have air, water and food. I'm okay. I don't need anything else.

8. Create a schedule

I'm already on one— which contains nothing but sleeping.

9. Read a book

I've read all of them.

10. Watch out for other mental health symptoms

I am suffering from a very serious mental disorder and I don't need to watch out for it because this illness is apparent, and it's consuming me, leaving me hollow.

This site is so ridiculous! I don't need its advice. I need options that are less stupid.

10:45 pm

I counted the seconds for the morning to break through. I felt better in the mornings than in the vile nights. So in the end, I didn't sleep and saved up my sleep for the afternoon.

I don't want to go away from you, but now I have to.
Pleasant dreams.

I tore the page on which I'd made mistakes, yet on the new page, I realized I'd made the same mistake.

1 AUGUST, 2021

SUNDAY

How to love life when life departs?
Winter is cold and even colder for the weak ones.

My thoughts are like a traffic jam— I never seem to get my way out of the traffic. The situation felt monotonous, because I was stuck. And my thoughts came as 'unwelcomed guests.'

There are words: unexpected, unforeseen, unanticipated.
But there are two facets of the word 'unexpected.'
One meaning holds when something unexpected great happens, and the other holds when something unexpected, disastrous happens.

If only had I been prepared for the fate for me, it would have been harmless. It was so sudden that's why it was dangerous.

7:06 am

My anxiety is as bad as getting hit on the head.

I moved my schools and I can't be happier as the schools are closed. I hate, hate, hate school more than anything in my entire life. It is agony to go to school. I can't stand it there. I hope that they never ever open.

2 AUGUST, 2021

MONDAY

I rode my bicycle early in the morning, accompanied by my mother as she had insisted me to go for bicycling with her. And for the first time in my life, my agonized soul was at tranquility. But I was sure, it wouldn't last long.

I did lay on the bench and gazed at the clouds passing. The breeze tossed my brown hair. I finally turned my face towards the sun and slept while its fierce rays fell upon my skin. Sometimes, I get the feeling as if I'm watching my life go on rather than living it.

Finally, I got up and plucked out a rose. I placed it in my mother's hair.

"The flower looks appealing on you," I said.

"O I'm an old woman now."

And it was true as I could spot grey hair strands in my mother's hair.

She held my hand and we walked in the park for a while, silently. Finally, we retired back home.

10:16 am

I got a sufficient sleep today. I had transformed back into a human being and not an owl.

I had sent my uncle an e-mail to order me a book. So he sent it today. It was the book *Emma* by Jane Austen, which I had wanted to read for a long time. I placed the book on my shelf and reached out to the kitchen. My mother made tea for herself and I put jam and mayonnaise simultaneously on two loaves of bread. I wrapped the bread and poured milk into a glass.

I was always fond of milk and chocolate my whole life. I loved noodles too. I hope that my father orders my favorite Hakka noodles in dinner tonight. Most of the time he orders pizza, which I don't like much. Plus, me and my father seem to avoid each other, only speaking when it's really necessary.

My mother has started to sleep with me for the past few days due to my nightmares. I would have happily forbidden her not to sleep with me, but I had no option as I didn't have anybody and it was stressful to sleep alone all nights. So, I invited her.

My mother is sometimes such a kiddo. I have always loved my mother more than my father.

I lifted my cat and put her on my lap. She purred. Now I will write 'thank you' to my uncle for the book.

1:08 pm

I discovered I'd developed a sore throat and it was hurting already. It was bad. I started to think how each day, my life was gifted with a problem or a woe. That my life could never be at peace, even for a day. In the evening, it was the same disaster— it was either a fight with my father, or calling my brother a *jerk, psycho* and other words without noticing my father could hear and I would get reprimanded for the same.

Life is never painless. That's why I sleep all the time. And sleeping is nothing but escaping the pain and it's the best thing. No thoughts of the awful past, my past mistakes or just anything from the past came there.

6:06 pm

I thought how I was running and never taking a break. Running meant doing work. And the more I started to complete my work, the longer it grew.

I wasn't making time for myself, I realized. I'd put each thing before me.

4 AUGUST, 2021

WEDNESDAY

Accepting the truth was like jumping from the stars to the earth. And I'd never in my life forsake the stars.

Accepting is easy, expecting is hard. And I chose the hard way.

Some of the few benefits of a broken heart are— that I can place the two broken pieces on my back, in form of a beautiful pair of wings, then fly higher and higher.

My heart had been trapped, exploited and finally been relentlessly thrown away. And all by means of words, this lovely crime had taken place. The words were etched into my heart and death could make it all go away.

9:00 pm

I remembered those words I'd said to *him* once:

If you hurt me, it doesn't matter. My mind and my spirit would never give me the strength to hate you, and I'd rather hate myself because I love you so much.

11:35 pm

It was a mortification to cry for someone who didn't spend a single second thinking about me. And yet, I had spent months sobbing over someone who had absolutely nothing to do with me.

But it didn't matter anyway. I wanted to water my pillow every night with those trifling amounts of my tender tears.

No pain could match the moment when *he* ignored me completely. He walked away from my life as if a train— departing from the old station to another station. Then there's me, who runs hastily to catch the fleeing train, to board it and to live my life. With all blood and flesh, I hasten towards it, panting. Yet no matter what, due to contrary winds, the train departs right in front of my eyes. And I couldn't even get my feet to move, as my feet were utterly stuck to the ground. My mind bent into complete blankness. It had vanished, right there.

6 AUGUST, 2021

FRIDAY

My deep slumber was broken by the sound of alarm. I got up, did the necessary tasks and studied Shakespeare.

I still feel tired and perhaps I suffer from a disorder called 'I feel tired every time for no reason (IFTEFNR).'

The freezing numbness expanded in my entire body. So I lay inert in my bed and waited for time to pass as much as it could.

My cousin had come over and I seem to know her for a really long time. Of course, she'll have to share my room as we didn't live in a mansion or something.

I hated visitors in my house. I didn't like the idea of them sharing the room with me. But alas, I have to. Also, my mother has started to get too much on my nerves and the worst thing about her is that she passes judgement in almost everything and was often forgetful. But, in spite of all, I preferred my mother to my stern father.

Me and my father have started 'talking' to each other once again, and I think it's safe to say that we both are not deadly enemies right now.

I don't like to be around people. I love to be all by myself.

Goodnight.

8 AUGUST, 2021

SUNDAY

'Why am I here?'
The thought which came across my mind today when I'd woken up. It didn't make sense for me to be here.

For all I knew, I was living in the daylight and dying in the moonlight. And I was not living, I was alive. That's all.

I wanted to do nothing today or buy some good novels from the web. But as usual, I was interrupted. My cousin forced me to go out with her, and it all went downhill from there.

"Come on! You barely go out. The staying in the bed—not going out, is just not healthy. No friends... No interests... No makeup... abstaining from taking food, not taking bath—AND THAT HAIR!" she shouted. "Women at least make sure their hair is perfect even when their life isn't. But you— above all! The little brat!"

"Stop it. I'm okay with the way it is." I sighed.
It wouldn't help if I cared or brushed my hair or just became more organized. I wanted things mostly my way— the unhealthiest way— to be slothful all the time. And little did my weak body allow me to get out of the bed.

"SAMAIRA!" she exclaimed. "If you're in this— terrible state, maybe it's a passing phase... not after days, but at least after months you'd be fine. Everybody has these days—"

"Then I'm not everybody," I interrupted to correct her. "It's not a passing phase either. The anxiety rules over me. I can never be normal again. And... when I'm happy, I see *those* words. They can never be erased from my mind."

"Which words?" she insisted.

And then I thought I was in a beautiful trouble.

"Uh— um—," I hesitated.
I was reluctant to accept that some way or another, I'd been *injured* by someone.

"Just some stupid words. I just ignore them," I lied. "They're nothing— just nothing okay?"

"Fine, if that's what suits you. You are harming yourself, and you're the one responsible for your deeds."

She let it go and went out of the room in a huff. Finally, I went to the kitchen and made milk for myself. I poured milk and added sugar in the glass and drank it.

I tried not to think of her advice.

11 AUGUST, 2021

WEDNESDAY

Just as the sun ascends, a tear from my eye gently descends.
For even the sun, the symbol of both vigor and life, couldn't
sway me with its zealous energy.

The morning rays pierced through the window and fell upon
my face, drenched with tears. It was then dark inside, as I
had hidden under the blanket, cuddling dismally with my
pillows. I was relentlessly shedding tears on the bedsheet,
making a stain on it.

Tears were the carriers of the hurt in my body.

I howled finally, screeched and screeched in excessive pain,
as if I could lose my voice due to the high-pitched cry.

The origin of the aches were my own thoughts; I screeched
on the thought of *his* words, the most painful words.
It was happening all over again.

That one night, happened every single night.
Even after months, I felt those words carved in my memory.
I remembered it— the voice, the words— crystal clear.
And it felt like I was going to perish from the coldest of the
coldest winters— my whole body and my vocal cords were
frozen, and I couldn't even cry for help and nothing could
save me.

Outward forces tore us apart, time changed things and
love faded.

Love goes up, never comes down.

I started to recall those days with *him*. I clearly remember the date: *19ᵗʰ of September, 2020.*

We met on the coldest nights yet I could feel the warmest presence of him. And all those empty nights filled by his presence. We came from different streams of water yet emerged in the same ocean of love.

It was 2 am in the night, he was giving me very hard kisses all over my mouth as I had asked him to kiss me on my lips and just... everywhere. He said I was being very *naughty.* He then tapped his cheek, his lips curled in dejection, as he hadn't received a single kiss and had eagerly stolen all the kisses from me. So I put my warm hand around his cold neck and felt the warmth, the bliss, even in the coldness.

I looked deeply into his eyes and the only contentment originated from his eyes. Although his eyes were black, I espied a bright sun in his eyes. And whenever he would look away or was absent, the sun would set, and the night would make its appearance.

Finally, I locked my lips with his. I figured we both were very much blind in love. I felt as if I was frosted with ice and he was going to melt me with his words. His words touched me more than the kisses.

I was on a journey with him to the stars.

I started to kiss his warm fingertips one by one and he reclined his head on my shoulder as if he were about to sleep. He was tired.

I had spent just three hours with him and yet it felt like days. Or in the other way, the moment was almost as if the speed of light, so fast yet so bright.

Moments like these could not be preserved, but my memory preserved them. The sky was dark and the only light came out of his eyes.

How could I want more? When I had everything— him.

I finally said to him, "Let's run away."

"How do you want to run away, by car or metro?" he asked.

"No car, no metro. Let's run away by a bus and let's run away from everything, to a place somewhere alone, just me and you." I replied solemnly.

I told him that I wanted him badly, even more than I wanted that night to never end.

We had planned the whole future, when to do this and that. He promised that he would marry me, and I had everything planned with him. But little did I know that our future was going to end *too soon*, all of that.

It wasn't even years or decades that we were together. Just seven months and yet lasting as long as the lifetime of a star.

It was dawn then. I had fallen asleep on his shoulder while I had clung to his chest with my arms.

At length, he got up, kissed me on the cheek, looked at me with an incomprehensible curiosity and departed home.

I was still sleepy. I got up and made my way to the bed. I shut my eyes and felt the hollow numbness taking over my whole body. Time passed slowly. After a while I got a call, I suddenly knew from whom it was. It was from him.

After I'd received the call, it changed my life forever. His father got to know all of it, not leaving a single thing. He caught him just as he had entered the house, and he berated and beat him up sorely.

It was done— the last page of the chapter of our love had been inscribed by destiny. The journey to the stars was over.

On the call, he said he'd never return, as he couldn't take it anymore and would vanish thoroughly from my life.

He sounded so irritated with me. His words came out hard and painful as if he were joking instead of being serious. But he wasn't; I knew what he meant. I couldn't yet make out what my fault was.

He made his last words to me by asserting that he was very happy when he was single, when I wasn't a part of his life. And then he ended the call in a haste.

He made it so clear, leaving it so unclear for me. Each word made me feel more and more hollow in the chest.

I stared blankly at the black screen of the phone in my hand. Everything was doomed. Not only had the call ended, but something even more—

My everything had ended.

20 AUGUST, 2021

FRIDAY

Every time my parents uttered *his* name, I'd completely lose it.

"Look what he's done to you! A green leaf like you has turned into a brown one! What harms he has inflicted upon you!" my mother shouted. "That one idiot— one man in the whole world— weeping for him!"

Then both my mother and father would start taking his name, which felt as if a hundred needles were pricking against my skin, or like my head was going to explode. It felt like I wanted to jump off a building. I couldn't stand hearing his name.

"STOP— STOP TAKING HIS NAME!" I howled. "Or I'll *just*—," I refrained myself from saying the last words. I was so angry and so sad at the same time.

Since then, an unforgiving antagonism had arisen between me and my parents. We never seem to be calm or just— get along well.

On top of all, it was the stupid depression. I didn't like depression back and it liked me. This rejection makes it sad, so it clings on to me even more. If I'd start loving my depression, it would leave me, just like everyone else does.

1 SEPTEMBER, 2021

WEDNESDAY

Time with healing hand which mended all wounds, could not heal my mourning and the unhappiness of all those months because of love.

My mother described me as completely delusional, paranoid and demented for the past seven months. As time passed, she could certainly see what little improvement I made. It had become apparent. So she decided to take me to a psychiatrist.

I truly believed it would not help me in any way if I took therapy or just visited the clinic, for it would only be for deranged people like me.

After much argument with my mother, reluctantly, I had to go with her. There, I attended counselling sessions and received some antidepressants, sleeping pills, pills for anxiety, while others for panic attacks, as I would get these terrible chest pains which came and went, and it felt like I was having a heart attack.

During psychotherapy sessions, the psychiatrist asked, "What do you think might be the root of your anxiety and depression?"

Him.

"It's the past. Everything from the past keeps coming back to me. Or— the thoughts of the people with whom I had encountered a bad experience with... they are persisting," I said nonchalantly. "As much as I did brood over the past, the more did my health seem to collapse."

"Hmm. I see. You say *rumination* takes up most of your vigor?"

"Yes," I agreed. If it wasn't for rumination, I'd have been much better.

After being on medication for a week, he asked me if I had experienced any side effects. And I had. In the first week, I experienced excessive sleepiness and after a few days I felt even more depressed. Most of the time I'd forget to take my sleeping pills and consequently would stay up the whole night.

After two weeks, I started to feel better. At least I didn't feel anxious; one good thing came out of it. I didn't brood over the future the whole time, of how terrible it was going to turn, or how *he* was going to have the best days of his life with everything he ever wanted, and how I'd suffer and remain in the state of delirium my whole life.

Then I remembered all those times— when I didn't see myself a particular way, until *he* saw me in the similar way. If he saw me as worthless, I started to perceive myself the same way, as I was in thrall to him.

17 SEPTEMBER, 2021

FRIDAY

Love and death sometimes share the same path— they seem to have completely different meanings but are eventually the same.
I couldn't rebuke love. For such a rapturous sentiment could not lead to a cruel death. And yet, love had the power to affect as much as that of death.

The magnet that attracts, may repel vigorously when pulled away.

Once and for all, I contemplated the time when he was the medicine to all my unhappiness, now for all the unhappiness caused by him I was receiving medicines.

How all those nights I used to sit in my room, helpless, staring emptily at the pills in my hand, desperate to take them. I thought an overdose would certainly aid my troubled mind, as I saw death as the only end for all the pain.

Ah death, end of anxiety.

SEPTEMBER 18, 2021

SATURDAY

The winter is tempestuous and we need fire. Don't make someone your fire for winters as they can be absent and you'll die out of frost.

From the happiest nights to the most torturous nights, the most captivating sight turned into the most terrifying sight—

Despite everything, in the end,
More than love, for dignity she cared.

POEMS

POEM-I

My eyes are criminals for the chief crime of love,
And I am the victim of love.

The origin of the wound of love
Courses from the eyes till the heart,
As eyes carry the beauty's image to the heart.

My eyes informed the heart,
Then both my heart and eyes
Deluded my mind for love,
And alas, I became a victim of my own eyes.

Your eyes are black, yet I see no darkness,
I see infinite light, as bright as the heavens.
At length, Cupid pierced my heart,
And my heart surrendered to such a vision like you.

You mended all my wounds by your healing eye,
And after all the persisting nights,
Day did emerge inside me.

O I had lost myself that minute,
Just as the night loses itself to the day.

POEM-II

I blame nor time, nor fortune nor my actions,
I blame you, Lord, for all the mishaps.

O Lord, you created the universe,
Thus, I blame you for creating such a fine beauty,
And for presenting this beauty in front of my eyes,
That no resistance may suffice;
Leading me to become a prey of my own chase.

I blame you, delusory heart,
For making this poison appear like chocolate.

Ah, I can't inculpate the Lord or my emotions,
And I must blame my eyes,
As they lead me to the unhappy decision
Of falling in love with you.

POEM-III

Your eyes are ink black,
And so does my future remain black,
Like an abyss of despair.

All I see is black— my perspective black,
My thoughts also black,
That I see nothing but a wretched life ahead.

To save me from this never-ending pain,
I shall make this black future white,
By turning this miserable life to a painless demise,
And setting this life full of torment
Into a trouble-free zone:
Heaven.

POEM-IV

I'm so scared, he has changed so much,
He is so strange now...
When I ask him what's wrong with him,
He starts to blame me

The change in his behavior makes my heart shiver,
As if sending waves of distress through my veins.

It feels like he has aged a decade,
Even though he has aged just a month.

Although his tongue speaks his love for me,
His eyes reveal hostility.
Hence his words contradict his eyes.
As words may seductively mislead,
But the eyes uncloak the truth.

POEM-V

O Foolish love, I must censure you,
For I love the one who scorns me.
O unsteady love, for all the delights loaned,
In the end, we reimburse it with mortal sorrows.
O love, you make me discard the truth
When it's put right in front of my eyes.
O love, why do you get me hurt a thousand times
Than to just end me with one death.
O fortune, you send outward forces
To obstruct the love between me and my lover.

The climb of the hill of love takes long,
But the fall is rapid.

Almost died because of love, still survived.

For the lord of beauty, the lover's heart
Must toil and serve as a slave.

O blurred eyesight, I perceive a bark of wood
As a lustrous jewel.

POEM-VI

I am good
I am fine
I am content
I am thankful
Until your name is spoken from someone's mouth,
And so it reaches my ear, the sound of your name,
That it makes me stand still,
Then slowly sink to the ground,
Making me shudder
With fingers digging deep into my head,
Ripping out my hair relentlessly.

And then I realize the destruction
In just hearing the name of you.

POEM-VII

This is the act of the final play—
From now on I'm fully yours!
I choose to be with you.

I am a caterpillar who refuses to turn into a butterfly,
As I am enveloped within a cocoon
Of delusions and fantasy.

The moon can be influenced by the sun's beams,
But the sun can never be influenced by the moon's.

POEM-VIII

If this is the life I get— to live without you,
I shall set myself free— to bring ease to my soul,
I shall gladly place myself in the hands of death,
As the dolor etched into my grieving breast
Is worse than death itself.

Why would I shed a thousand painful tears,
When one painless death
Can discard my soul from my body?

POEM-IX

If I died,
I wouldn't have to think of him,
I wouldn't have to be unhappy,
I would never let anyone abuse me,
I wouldn't have to think of the ghastly future,
I wouldn't have to see him in his lover's arms.

He's going to live his life, I'm not.
And I'm happy, not for him, but for myself.

POEM-X

My lover was a bright sky
Now obscured by the clouds of death.
Alas, I can't understand it, I can't believe it,
I can't accept it,
As you have slipped away from my hand
Without any warning.

POEM-XI

I shall state death being the ultimate end,
But there are two ends in life:
Either a long road of love or a deep anguish.

When the road of love comes to an end,
Anguish is produced,
And when the anguish comes to an end,
Joy is induced.
But my melancholy after being abandoned by you
Never seems to come to an end.

POEM-XII

As long as I'm relying upon the delusion, I'm safe,
It's the truth which makes me squeal in pain.

They say the truth shall set us free,
But that's a lie; it only makes me a prisoner
To my own delusions.

POEM-XIII

Pain is not pain,
Pain helps us to learn from sorrows,
Pain makes us see a better version of ourselves,
Pain makes us find our true selves.

The most beautiful arts and literature
Are inspired through feeling pain.

The captivating butterfly is born out of the cocoon,
And so does improvement emerge from pain.

Happiness comes from pain.

Pain has more to do with growth than misery.

POEM-XIV

I give this orchid to you,
It is as beautiful as you are!
I didn't cut it off.
It's so sad when people ruin flowers
Instead of taking pleasure in their beauty.

The scent of an alluring flower
Altered into the scent of a poison—
And I have a feeling that it is killing me.
He said I shouldn't worry...

My heart is breaking, it hurts so much;
Is it a disease or is it because of you?

POEM-XV

To my dear love:
Life with you isn't just life, it's a fairytale!
Your charm had subjugated me long time back,
And I tried to resist it,
But what power can exceed that of beauty.

I'm like a tulip, drooped within the route of time,
Due to the fiery rays of the irate sun (angry lover).
The tulip didn't obtain any water (of love)
From its gardener (lover).

Alas, I never thought that innocent flowers
Could betray a person,
Until I received the flowers from you.

POEM-XVI

You must give back the thing
Which you once received,
For the most captivating tulip shall lose its dye,
And the most ravishing blossoms and dandelions
Shall surrender themselves to the barbaric winter,
As the birth of the spring shall bend
Into the deteriorating hands of winter.

Yet above all, I refuse this act of decay,
As one thing is unvanquished:
The memory of your alluring eyes,
To which the winter had to bow.

O what power shall seasons have on my memory,
When the only thing that shall make my memory
Deteriorate and submit, shall be by death itself.

POEM-XVII

There is an oddity in the world of ours:
It began like a very simple love story,
And ended in an appalling tragedy.

You were as good as the month of spring,
Yet as vile as the month of winter.

Either the unattractive flower,
Or the most beautiful flower of spring,
Each flower has to lose its beauty,
As winter spares none.

From the blooms of the spring,
To the shedding and wilting of the winter.
O ruthless winter!

POEM-XVIII

My dear love, my heart which you threw away
Is now forever lost,
Yet I assure you, your heart
Rests eternally with me,
And shall be kept safe with me,
Till life remains in me.

So, I say, you shall never be able to love again,
Or offer your heart to anybody else,
As I have your heart.

I forgive you but I can never forgive myself.

Time who healed the wound
Had itself thrust the wound.

Ah, dear love, you are the pristine prize desired by all,
But from the inside,
You have been used and exploited sorely.

POEM-XIX

Beauty is a veil,
Which conceals all the foulness that lies within.

When you are with me,
You put a mask on your face,
Thus disguised, you embrace me in your arms,
In a way that no other feeling can surpass
The bliss of your touch,
As if I were floating on the clouds of heaven.

But when you reveal your face,
A countenance so repulsive I see.
Still, despite all, my mind forgets all your flaws,
As once the poison of love is spread in the veins,
It cannot be undone.

Sometimes the gentle touch of hand
Affects more than beauty.

POEM-XX

O nasty time, will you take away my everything?
O time, you are cold-blooded, rigid and callous!
O cruel time, don't be so gluttonous,
Spit out my lover which you have engulfed.

Time doesn't seem to open its jaws,
And has already consumed my beloved.
So I shall keep my lover's memory
Unconsumed by time.

POEM-XXI

Just like after a war
All the resources of a country are depleted,
In my war against time, my energy is also expended.
As time has done a major crime:
It has consumed the most precious part of my heart.

In the end, even after losing against time,
I won, by keeping my lover's memory
Unconquered by time.
And time has surrendered to me,
As I have not made my lover's memory governed by it.

POEM-XXII

O merciless time,
You have the competence
To eliminate things within your route,
But my memory will not give you the strength
To dominate and change.

My memory does the most beautiful job
Of preserving the loveliest creature, my lover,
As if a sacred painting is preserved.

My memory's intensity exceeds
Time's giant and dominant power,
And my memory says to time: 'I forbid it time,
Kneel before me! My power exceeds yours.'
My memory of you sits untouched
By time's ruthless hand.

O the flower is my lover, the roots being my memory,
And no wind, no rain, no storm can affect this flower.

A withered flower with brown leaves.
Yet the memory of you is like a green leaf
Grown out from the wilted flower.

POEM-XXIII

My thoughts are like the sun,
Consuming me with its fiery heat,
And those thoughts of sorrowful love,
Chasing me everywhere I go.

Being abandoned in love
Is like being in the flaming sun,
But being abused in love
Is like death, or being in the coldest winter.

Love's sorrows surpass all sorrows.

The ink black color of your eyes painted the whole sky.
The morning never arose,
It was irrevocably the night sky,
Just like the depressive frame of my mind,
Which remains at one pole constantly.

POEM-XXIV

My poetry and your worth
Can never share the same road,
As you are ugly in reality,
But my poetry makes you alluring.

Anger is destructive,
Yet my anger for you lasts not hours, days or months,
But measly seconds.

Even when you promised the respectful love,
You still laugh with your friends
About how dull and oversensitive I am,
And your friends tell you
To leave a worthless woman like me,
And to my surprise, dear love, you agree with them,
And admit how despicable I am.

Ah, dear love, if it takes just seconds
For you to change your mind about me,
Then, I say, desert me proudly,
So I can find a humble gentleman for me,
Whose virtuous thought of me lasts a man's lifetime,
Not wretched days.

POEM-XXV

September turns to October,
And so does your perspective of me turns
From worthy to contemptible.
It takes you just a month to change your mind.

February bends into October,
Still loving you for eight months while you are far away.

O unfriendly lover, you laugh with your friends
While I'm dying inside,
And your friends and family
Shall always be your top priority,
While I, your doleful lover,
Shall be the least consequential.

POEM-XXVI

When she holds you
You look happier in her arms,
And you both laugh while looking at me

She doesn't love you for making me jealous,
But to destroy me completely.
And you let it happen,
As if I were forgotten within a week.

You could have just rejected me long before
To save me from these deadly pains,
Because now my life is horrible than before.

Letting me go through torture
Than to discard me at once
Induces harms you can't comprehend.

You pledged you will never go to her,
But still when I observe your mischievous hidden love:
See you enjoying with her,
Touching every part of her skin,
Traumatizing my poor heart
For your own good pleasure,

That how inferior I felt of her,
How worthless I felt,
That I wasn't blessed with a single love
Which didn't injure me.

The more pains you give to me
The more my fragile heart is greedy for you.

When you hurt me,
I hurt myself a thousand times more badly.

She was happy for her triumph over me,
And I were now relieved
Of the agony of being with you.

When she gazes at me while holding you,
She was happy, I was happy.

POEM-XXVII

How can a situation like this be more blissful?
I am in another state, you are in another.

Too far you are from me
That no scent of yours is to be felt here.
No sign of your voice,
Or the footsteps indicating that you have come.
Ah, agonized house!

Still, I shall wait for you,
Delude myself that you will come,
Even though you will never come back home,
And you never did; you always stayed the same.

POEM- XXVIII

When shall you come?
Your thoughts come everywhere with me,
And your memory makes the equal balance
Of ache and joy.

The pleasant illusions of you
Are like a charming prince standing at my door,
(The door being the entry to my mind)
And yet, I do not dare
To open the door (to think of you),
As your illusions may seem enticing,
But they bring waves of severe distress:
The reminder that I have lost you.

POEM-XXIX

You are not close to me,
And the only time we can get closer
Is through the wires.

As you have told me to wait for your call,
I shall sit near the telephone, waiting,
And let the tears flow tenderly down my cheek.

I feel thankful to the telephone,
As even when you are far,
The telephone does the lovely job
Of bringing you nearer to me.

Let nobody know or hear our secret conversation,
Let your voice be transported to me by the wires,
And slowly let the comfort from your voice
Be carried from the ears to my desperate breast,
And give relief to it,
Because no solace lies but in your voice.

POEM-XXX

You are the angel of death,
I can feel a strangeness in your behavior.

Each word spoken by you makes me shudder,
Which drives me to end my life once and for all,
So as to bring an end to this never-ending agony
Created by your words.

Words: as paltry as the sand,
As harmless as a bird sitting on a tree,
But the damage done by your trifling words
Is as much as a dagger piercing through me,
As dangerous as a wild wolf sitting at my door.

POEM-XXXI

The importance which I give to you
Is at the highest position in my heart.

My mind is the book,
Your words are the letters etched in the book.
Ah, I wish to efface your violent words
By an eraser which erases words,
But alas, these words are not written by graphite,
These words are written in fierce black ink,
That shall remain unaffected to any erase.

O your words shall rest on the book (my mind)
As long as life continues,
Or as long as my spirit forsakes my body.

POEM-XXXII

Our love is notorious,
There are no roses, no rings,
No jewelry, no ornaments,
Yet there is something
Which makes me feel wealthier
Than these mere things:
Just words said by you.
As your words send me waves
Of priceless and incomparable love,
That no wealth can buy the bliss of these words.

Words said by someone else's mouth
Seem trifling to me,
But when spoken from your mouth,
Seem serious to me,
As I give your words the utmost importance.

When all fades, your words remain.

POEM-XXXIII

If there's something darker than the sky, it's my mind.

My mind was inquired: 'O foolish mind,
What did you admire so much in the lover?'
And so did my mind make its answer, 'Eyes.'

Just as a rocket lifts off,
The sentiments of love tower high,
That both, at length reach the vacuum,
Where there's nothing but emptiness.

Love comes as a stranger, goes as a stranger.

SAMAIRA

About the Author

Samaira Singh is 16 years old and resides in New Delhi. *Rain* is her first novella, which includes poems.